QUICHES & FLANS

NOTES

Standard spoon measurements are used in all recipes

1 tablespoon = one 15 ml spoon
1 teaspoon = one 5 ml spoon
All spoon measures are level.

Fresh herbs are used unless otherwise stated. If unobtainable, substitute a bouquet garni of the equivalent dried herbs, or use dried herbs instead but halve the quantities stated.

Ovens and grills (broilers) should be preheated to the specified temperature or heat setting.

For all recipes, quantities are given in metric, imperial and American measures. Follow one set of measures only, because they are not interchangeable.

QUICHES & FLANS

Edited by
Deirdre Sadlier

Contents

**First published in hardcover in 1981
by Octopus Books Limited
59 Grosvenor Street, London W1**

This edition first published 1983

© 1981 Octopus Books Limited

ISBN 0 7064 2019 5

Produced by Mandarin Publishers Limited
22a Westlands Road
Quarry Bay, Hong Kong

Printed in Hong Kong

Front cover photography by Paul Williams

Frontispiece: APPLE AND HAZELNUT FLAN (PIE) *(page 67)*
(Photograph: Flour Advisory Bureau)

INTRODUCTION

Quiches and flans (pies) both consist of a shallow crisp base with a sweet or savoury filling, and providing endless variety for all kinds of meals and occasions.

The quiche originates from the Lorraine area of France, hence the famous 'Quiche Lorraine', an unsweetened pastry (dough) case (shell) filled with eggs, cream cheese and sometimes bacon. This is baked to set the filling and give the top a lovely golden colour, and traditionally is served as an hors d'oeuvre.

However, quiches and flans (pies) are also ideal for main meals, snacks, buffet parties and picnics. A savoury flan (pie) may be served hot with a variety of salads to give a tasty and nutritious meal. Sweet flans (pies) may be served hot or cold – alone, or with cream or custard.

The traditional base for a quiche is pastry (dough) but there are many variations, including potato or savoury biscuit (cracker) bases. Additional flavourings can be added to the dough; wholemeal (wholewheat) flour will give more texture and colour to the pastry (dough). For sweet flans (pies) there is even more scope as flavouring can be added to pastry (dough), sponge or biscuit (cracker) bases.

The appearance of the flan (pie) can be enhanced by the dish or tin (pan) used, there are many attractive ones available. Ovenproof, glazed earthenware dishes are particularly convenient as the flan (pie) or quiche can be cooked and served in them and, in addition to the traditional round shape, they come in squares, ovals and rectangles. A plain or fluted metal ring placed on a baking sheet serves equally well for cooking quiches and flans (pies), which can then be transferred to a plate or dish, as preferred. If a loose bottom tin (pan) is used, transferring to a plate is even easier as the base can be left under the flan (pie), which is then less likely to break. Individual dishes and tins (pans) make a change from one large dish and add novelty to the meal.

The recipes on the following pages give many ideas for savoury and sweet fillings to please all tastes. The quiche type, based on an egg custard, can be varied with almost any savoury food such as meat, fish, cheeses, vegetables, nuts, herbs and spices. The flan cases (pie shells) can also be filled with a sauce which has added ingredients and flavourings. Both are excellent ways of using up leftover food. Sweet flans (pies) may have custard or sauce fillings with sweet additions, or they may be based on fruit or cream. Some chilled flans (pies) include gelatine to help setting. Fruits in flans (pies) can be varied according to what is available or in season.

Most quiches and flans (pies) will freeze, either whole or in portions, but fruit toppings are best added after thawing. Flavourings and spices will become stronger during freezing so this should be considered when making a flan (pie) for storing in the freezer. A quiche or flan (pie) can be thawed in the refrigerator overnight or at room temperature for 2 to 4 hours. Cooked varieties can then be refreshed in the oven if desired.

If it is not convenient to freeze a complete flan (pie) it is worth making extra bases and freezing them in the dishes or tins (pans). Fillings can then be added quickly when required.

For those who have never explored further than a 'Quiche Lorraine', a new adventures begins overleaf and for those already converted many new ideas can be found.

Servings:

All the quiche and flan (pie) recipes will give 4 to 6 portions, but those in the Appetizers and Savouries section can be cut into 8 to 10 portions, depending on the other dishes to be served.

Baking pastry cases (pie shells):

In the recipes, all shortcrust pastry (pie dough) and richer pastry (dough) bases are cooked before adding the filling. See 'baking blind' below. This gives a crisper base. If the sides of the case (shell) become too brown while the filling is cooking, the whole flan (pie) or quiche can be covered with aluminium foil.

Acceptable results can still be achieved by filling an uncooked pastry case (pie shell) and baking for the time given in the recipe. A crisper base will be achieved if the dish or tin (pan) is placed on a baking sheet in the oven to concentrate the heat in this area.

To 'bake blind':

Line the flan case (pie shell) with a piece of greaseproof (wax) paper and fill with dried beans. Place in a preheated moderately hot oven (190°C/375°F, Gas Mark 5) for 10 minutes. Remove the beans and paper, then bake for a further 5 minutes. Leave to cool.

CHEESY VEGETABLE WHEATEN FLAN (PIE) *(page 31)*
(Photograph: Flour Advisory Bureau)

FLAN BASES

Basic Shortcrust Pastry (Pie Dough)

METRIC/IMPERIAL
175 g/6 oz plain flour
pinch of salt
40 g/1½ oz margarine
40 g/1½ oz lard
2–3 tablespoons water

AMERICAN
1½ cups all-purpose flour
pinch of salt
3 tablespoons margarine
3 tablespoons shortening
2–3 tablespoons water

Sift the flour and salt into a bowl. Rub in the margarine and lard (shortening) until the mixture resembles fine breadcrumbs. Add the water and mix to a firm dough. Knead on a lightly floured surface until smooth. Roll out the pastry (dough) and use to line a 20 cm/8 inch flan tin (pie pan).

Variations:
Cheese Pastry (Dough)
Add a pinch of cayenne pepper with the salt and stir in 50 g/2 oz (½ cup) grated cheese before adding the water to the rubbed in mixture.
Herb Pastry (Dough)
Add ½ teaspoon mixed herbs to the rubbed in mixture.
Curry Pastry (Dough)
Add 1 teaspoon curry powder to the dry ingredients.
Wholemeal Pastry (Wholewheat Dough)
In any of the above bases substitute 75 g/3 oz (¾ cup) wholemeal (wholewheat) flour for the same quantity of plain (all-purpose) flour.

Almond Pastry (Dough)

METRIC/IMPERIAL	AMERICAN
100 g/4 oz plain flour	1 cup all-purpose flour
pinch of salt	pinch of salt
50 g/2 oz ground almonds	$\frac{1}{2}$ cup ground almonds
50 g/2 oz butter	$\frac{1}{4}$ cup butter
50 g/2 oz caster sugar	$\frac{1}{4}$ cup sugar
1 egg	1 egg
2 egg yolks	2 egg yolks

Sift the flour and salt on to a board. Make a well in the centre and sprinkle in the ground almonds. Place the butter, egg, egg yolks and sugar in the well. Using the fingertips of one hand, gradually work the ingredients together starting from the middle and at the same time gradually drawing flour in from the sides. Knead lightly until smooth then leave to rest for one hour in a cool place.

Roll out the pastry (dough) and use to line a 20 cm/8 inch flan tin (pie pan) placed on a baking tray. Bake 'blind' (see page 8).

French Flan Pastry (Pie Dough)

METRIC/IMPERIAL	AMERICAN
100 g/4 oz plain flour	1 cup all-purpose flour
pinch of salt	pinch of salt
50 g/2 oz butter	$\frac{1}{4}$ cup butter
2 egg yolks	2 egg yolks
50 g/2 oz caster sugar	$\frac{1}{4}$ cup sugar

Sift the flour and salt on to a board. Make a well in the centre and place the butter, egg yolks and sugar in the well. Using the fingertips of one hand, gradually work the ingredients together starting from the middle and gradually drawing in flour from the sides. Knead lightly then leave to rest for one hour in a cool place.

Roll out the pastry (dough) and use to line a 20 cm/8 inch flan tin (pie pan) placed on a baking tray. Bake 'blind' (see page 8).

Cheese and Oat Flan Case (Pie Shell)

METRIC/IMPERIAL	AMERICAN
75 g/3 oz butter	6 tablespoons butter
150 g/5 oz rolled oats	1½ cups rolled oats
75 g/3 oz cheese, grated	¾ cup grated cheese

Melt the butter in a saucepan and stir in the oats and cheese. Mix well then press the mixture into a 20 cm/8 inch flan tin (pie pan). Chill in the refrigerator for 30 minutes, then bake in a preheated moderately hot oven (200°C/400°F, Gas Mark 6) for 15 to 20 minutes until golden brown. Cool before adding the filling.

Cornflake Crust Flan Case (Pie Shell)

METRIC/IMPERIAL	AMERICAN
75 g/3 oz cornflakes	3 cups cornflakes
50 g/2 oz butter	¼ cup butter
50 g/2 oz sugar	¼ cup sugar
1 tablespoon golden syrup	1 tablespoon maple syrup

Roughly crush the cornflakes in a bowl. Heat the butter, sugar and golden syrup (maple syrup) in a saucepan until melted. Pour over the cornflakes and mix thoroughly together.

Press the mixture firmly into a 20 cm/8 inch flan tin (pie pan), then chill or leave in a cool place to set.

Potato Pastry (Dough)

METRIC/IMPERIAL	AMERICAN
50 g/2 oz margarine	¼ cup margarine
100 g/4 oz self-raising flour	1 cup self-rising flour
salt	salt
100 g/4 oz mashed potatoes	½ cup mashed potatoes

Place the margarine in a bowl and beat until soft. Add the flour and salt and mix well. Add the potatoes and bind together. Knead on a lightly floured surface until smooth. Roll out the pastry (dough) and use to line a 20 cm/8 inch flan tin (pie pan). Bake 'blind' (see page 8).

APRICOT AND ALMOND FLAN (PIE) *(page 68) (Photograph: John West Foods)*

Biscuit Flan Case (Cracker Pie Shell)

METRIC/IMPERIAL	AMERICAN
175 g/6 oz plain digestive biscuits	1½ cups Graham crackers
75 g/3 oz butter	6 tablespoons butter
1 teaspoon caster sugar	1 teaspoon sugar

Place the digestive biscuits (Graham crackers) in a polythene (plastic) bag and crush with a rolling pin.

Melt the butter and sugar in a saucepan. Remove from the heat and add crushed biscuits (crackers). Mix well. Press firmly into a 20 cm/8 inch flan tin (pie pan). Leave in a cool place to set.

Variations:
Lemon Biscuit Case (Cracker Pie Shell)
Add the grated rind of 1 lemon to the crushed biscuits (crackers).

Ginger Biscuit Case (Cracker Pie Shell)
Use 175 g/6 oz (1½ cups) gingernut biscuits (gingersnap cookies) in place of the digestive biscuits (Graham crackers).

Nut Flan Case (Pie Shell)

METRIC/IMPERIAL	AMERICAN
50 g/2 oz margarine	¼ cup margarine
1 tablespoon demerara sugar	1 tablespoon brown sugar
100 g/4 oz chopped mixed nuts	1 cup chopped mixed nuts
100 g/4 oz self-raising flour	1 cup self-rising flour

Place the margarine, sugar and nuts in a bowl and beat together until pale and creamy. Add the flour and work into the mixture with the fingertips. Roll out thinly and use to line a 20 cm/8 inch flan tin (pie pan). Chill.

Shortbread Flan Case (Pie Shell)

METRIC/IMPERIAL
150 g/5 oz plain flour
pinch of salt
25 g/1 oz ground rice
50 g/2 oz caster sugar
100 g/4 oz butter

AMERICAN
1¼ cups all-purpose flour
pinch of salt
1 tablespoon ground rice
¼ cup sugar
½ cup butter

Sift the flour, salt and ground rice into a bowl and stir in the sugar. Add the butter and rub into the dry ingredients. Knead until well mixed. Chill in the refrigerator for about 30 minutes. Press the chilled dough into a 20 cm/8 inch flan tin (pie pan). Prick all over with a fork and bake in a preheated moderate oven (160°C/325°F, Gas Mark 3) for 30 to 40 minutes until golden. Cool.

Sponge Flan Case (Pie Shell)

METRIC/IMPERIAL
2 eggs
4 tablespoons caster sugar
1 tablespoon hot water
3 tablespoons plain flour
1 teaspoon baking powder
¼ teaspoon salt

AMERICAN
2 eggs
4 tablespoons sugar
1 tablespoon hot water
3 tablespoons all-purpose flour
1 teaspoon baking powder
¼ teaspoon salt

Place the eggs and sugar in a bowl and whisk until thick and creamy. Add the hot water then quickly fold in the sifted flour, baking powder and salt. Turn into a greased and floured 20 cm/8 inch flan tin (pie pan) and bake in a preheated moderately hot oven (200°C/400°F, Gas Mark 6) for 15 to 20 minutes. Turn out and cool on a wire rack.

APPETIZERS AND SAVOURIES

Tomato Quiche

METRIC/IMPERIAL
*1 × 20 cm/8 inch shortcrust or herb
  pastry case (see page 10)*
Filling:
*350 g/12 oz tomatoes, thinly sliced
1 small onion, chopped
1 teaspoon chopped basil
1 teaspoon chopped parsley
1 teaspoon thyme
salt
freshly ground black pepper
2 tablespoons boiling water
1 egg
250 ml/8 fl oz milk*
Garnish:
*tomato slices
parsley*

AMERICAN
*1 × 8 inch basic pie dough or herb
  shell (see page 10)*
Filling:
*1½ cups thinly sliced tomatoes
1 small onion, chopped
1 teaspoon chopped basil
1 teaspoon chopped parsley
1 teaspoon thyme
salt
freshly ground black pepper
2 tablespoons boiling water
1 egg
1 cup milk*
Garnish:
*tomato slices
parsley*

Place the tomatoes, onion, basil, parsley, thyme, salt and pepper to taste, and water in a saucepan. Simmer for 5 to 6 minutes or until the vegetables are soft, then cool.

Beat together the egg and milk, then add to the tomato mixture. Pour into a prepared flan case (pie shell) and place in a preheated moderate oven (180°C/350°F, Gas Mark 4) for 35 to 40 minutes until the filling is set and golden. Garnish with the tomato and parsley and serve hot or cold.

TOMATO QUICHE *(Photograph: Milk Marketing Board)*

Quiche Lorraine

METRIC/IMPERIAL

1 × 20 cm/8 inch shortcrust pastry
  flan case (see page 10)
Filling:
175 g/6 oz streaky bacon, derinded
  and chopped
2 eggs
2 egg yolks
150 ml/¼ pint single cream
150 ml/¼ pint milk
salt
freshly ground black pepper
50 g/2 oz Gruyère cheese, grated

AMERICAN

1 × 8 inch basic pie dough shell (see
  page 10)
Filling:
9 fatty bacon slices, derinded and
  chopped
2 eggs
2 egg yolks
⅔ cup light cream
⅔ cup milk
salt
freshly ground black pepper
½ cup grated Gruyère cheese

Fry the bacon in its own fat in a frying pan (skillet) over a gentle heat until brown. Put the bacon into the prepared flan case (pie shell).

Place the eggs, egg yolks and cream in a bowl and beat together. Stir in the milk, and add salt and pepper to taste. Pour the mixture over the bacon and sprinkle with the grated cheese.

Bake in a preheated moderately hot oven (190°C/375°F, Gas Mark 5) for 25 to 30 minutes, until golden. Remove from the oven and leave to rest for 10 minutes before serving.

Mushroom Quiche

METRIC/IMPERIAL	AMERICAN
1 × 20 cm/8 inch shortcrust pastry flan case (see page 10)	1 × 8 inch basic pie dough shell (see page 10)
Filling:	**Filling:**
50 g/2 oz butter	$\frac{1}{4}$ cup butter
1 onion, chopped	1 onion, chopped
500 g/1 lb mushrooms, sliced	4 cups sliced mushrooms
1 tablespoon chopped parsley	1 tablespoon chopped parsley
salt	salt
freshly ground black pepper	freshly ground black pepper
3 eggs	3 eggs
120 ml/4 fl oz single cream	$\frac{1}{2}$ cup light cream
50 g/2 oz Cheddar cheese, grated	$\frac{1}{2}$ cup grated Cheddar cheese

Melt the butter in a large frying pan (skillet), add the onion and mushrooms and fry gently for 5 minutes. Remove from the heat and stir in the parsley and salt and pepper to taste.

Beat together the eggs, cream and cheese, then stir the mixture into the mushrooms and onions. Pour into the prepared flan case (pie shell).

Bake in a preheated moderately hot oven (200°C/400°F, Gas Mark 6) for 35 to 40 minutes. Serve hot or cold.

Egg Mayonnaise Quiche

METRIC/IMPERIAL	AMERICAN
1 × 20 cm/8 inch shortcrust or herb pastry flan case (see page 10)	1 × 8 inch basic pie dough or herb shell (see page 10)
Filling:	**Filling:**
300 ml/$\frac{1}{2}$ pint mayonnaise	1$\frac{1}{4}$ cups mayonnaise
1 large garlic clove, crushed	1 large garlic clove, crushed
4 tablespoons chopped fresh basil	4 tablespoons chopped fresh basil
3 hard-boiled eggs	3 hard-cooked eggs
Garnish:	**Garnish:**
1 hard-boiled egg, sliced	1 hard-cooked egg, sliced
6 parsley sprigs	6 parsley sprigs

Mix together the mayonnaise, garlic and basil in a bowl.

Finely chop the eggs and place in the prepared flan case (pie shell). Pour over the mayonnaise mixture and chill. Garnish with the egg slices and parsley.

Olive Savoury Flan (Pie)

METRIC/IMPERIAL

1 × 20 cm/8 inch shortcrust pastry case
  (or line Swiss roll tin, 17.5 × 27.5 cm/
  7 × 11 inches) (see page 10)

Filling:

350 g/12 oz tomatoes, sliced

150 ml/¼ pint double cream

1 egg

salt

freshly ground black pepper

100 g/4 oz cheese slices, cut into
  triangles

8 stuffed green olives, sliced

AMERICAN

1 × 8 inch basic pie dough shell (or
  line jelly roll pan, 7 × 11 inches)
  (see page 10)

Filling:

1½ cups sliced tomatoes

⅔ cup heavy cream

1 egg

salt

freshly ground black pepper

¼ lb cheese slices, cut into triangles

8 stuffed green olives, sliced

Arrange the tomato slices in the prepared flan case (pie shell). Beat together the cream, egg, and salt and pepper to taste, then pour over the tomatoes.

Top with the cheese and olives, then place in a preheated hot oven (220°C/425°F, Gas Mark 7) for 35 to 40 minutes. Serve hot or cold.

Cheese and Pineapple Flan (Pie)

METRIC/IMPERIAL

1 × 20 cm/8 inch shortcrust or cheese
  pastry flan case (see page 10)

Filling:

50 g/2 oz butter

50 g/2 oz plain flour

300 ml/½ pint milk

50 g/2 oz cheese, grated

¼ teaspoon mustard

salt and pepper

4 tablespoons crushed pineapple,
  drained

AMERICAN

1 × 8 inch basic pie dough or cheese
  shell (see page 10)

Filling:

¼ cup butter

½ cup all-purpose flour

1¼ cups milk

½ cup grated cheese

¼ teaspoon mustard

salt and pepper

4 tablespoons crushed pineapple,
  drained

Melt the butter in a saucepan, then stir in the flour and cook for 1 minute, stirring continuously. Remove from the heat and gradually blend in the milk. Return to the heat, and cook, stirring continuously, until the mixture thickens.

Remove from the heat and add the grated cheese, mustard and salt and pepper to taste. Stir in the pineapple and mix well together. Cool, then pour into the prepared flan case (pie shell). Serve chilled.

OLIVE SAVOURY FLAN (PIE) *(Photograph: Olives from Spain)*

Herb Cream Cheese Quiche

METRIC/IMPERIAL

1 × 20 cm/8 inch shortcrust or herb
 pastry flan case (see page 10)
Filling:
15 g/½ oz gelatine
2 tablespoons water
5 tablespoons milk
1 egg yolk
1 teaspoon mixed herbs
salt
freshly ground black pepper
100 g/4 oz soft cream cheese
½ teaspoon grated lemon rind
150 ml/¼ pint double cream

AMERICAN

1 × 8 inch basic pie dough or herb
 shell (see page 10)
Filling:
2 tablespoons gelatin
2 tablespoons water
5 tablespoons milk
1 egg yolk
1 teaspoon mixed herbs
salt
freshly ground black pepper
½ cup soft cream cheese
½ teaspoon grated lemon rind
⅔ cup heavy cream

Soak the gelatine in the water for 3 minutes. Heat the milk gently and stir in the gelatine until dissolved.

Place the egg yolk and herbs in a bowl with salt and pepper to taste and mix together, then add to the gelatine mixture.

Blend in the cheese, and leave to cool. Whip the cream until thick and fold into the cheese mixture. Pour into the prepared flan case (pie shell) and chill before serving.

Asparagus Barquettes

METRIC/IMPERIAL

6 individual round or oval wholemeal
 pastry cases (made from 175 g/6 oz
 flour – see page 10)
Filling:
2 eggs
6 tablespoons single cream
salt
freshly ground black pepper
1 × 350 g/12 oz can asparagus spears,
 drained
50 g/2 oz Gruyère cheese, grated

AMERICAN

6 individual round or oval wholewheat
 dough shells (made from 1½ cups
 flour – see page 10)
Filling:
2 eggs
6 tablespoons light cream
salt
freshly ground black pepper
1 × 12 oz can asparagus spears,
 drained
½ cup grated Gruyère cheese

Beat together the eggs, cream, and salt and pepper to taste. Divide the asparagus spears between the prepared pastry cases (pie shells) and pour the egg mixture over the top. Sprinkle with the cheese and place in a preheated moderately hot oven (200°C/400°F, Gas Mark 6) for 20 minutes until golden. Serve hot or cold.

Prawn (Shrimp) Quiche

METRIC/IMPERIAL

1 × 20 cm/8 inch shortcrust pastry
  flan case (see page 10)
Filling:
50 g/2 oz butter
1 onion, finely chopped
4 courgettes, sliced
275 g/10 oz shelled prawns
salt
freshly ground black pepper
pinch of ground nutmeg
120 ml/4 fl oz single cream
3 eggs
50 g/2 oz Cheddar cheese, grated

AMERICAN

1 × 8 inch basic pie dough shell (see
  page 10)
Filling:
$\frac{1}{4}$ cup butter
1 onion, finely chopped
4 zucchini, sliced
$1\frac{3}{4}$ cups shelled shrimp
salt
freshly ground black pepper
pinch of ground nutmeg
$\frac{1}{2}$ cup light cream
3 eggs
$\frac{1}{2}$ cup grated Cheddar cheese

Melt the butter in a saucepan and add the onion and courgettes (zucchini).
Fry gently until lightly brown, then stir in the prawns (shrimp) and cook
for about 3 minutes. Add salt and pepper to taste and the nutmeg, then
leave to cool.

Mix together the cream, eggs and cheese then stir in the prawn and
courgette (shrimp and zucchini) mixture. Pour into the prepared flan case
(pie shell) and bake in a preheated moderately hot oven (200°C/400°F,
Gas Mark 6) for 35 to 40 minutes. Serve hot.

Onion Quiche

METRIC/IMPERIAL

1 × 20 cm/8 inch shortcrust pastry flan
  case (see page 10)

Filling:

750 g/1½ lb large onions

40 g/1½ oz butter

3 eggs

250 ml/8 fl oz milk

salt

freshly ground black pepper

AMERICAN

1 × 8 inch basic pie dough shell (see
  page 10)

Filling:

1½ lb large onions

3 tablespoons butter

3 eggs

1 cup milk

salt

freshly ground black pepper

Peel the onions and slice thinly. Melt the butter in a heavy saucepan. Add the onions, cover and cook very slowly until they start to soften.

Beat together the eggs, milk, and salt and pepper to taste. Stir in the onions and pour the mixture into the prepared flan case (pie shell). Place in a preheated hot oven (220°C/425°F, Gas Mark 7) for 20 to 25 minutes until the filling is set and golden. Serve hot or cold.

Kipper and Egg Quiche

METRIC/IMPERIAL

1 × 20 cm/8 inch shortcrust pastry flan
  case (see page 10)

Filling:

175 g/6 oz kipper fillets

300 ml/½ pint water

2 hard-boiled eggs, chopped

225 g/8 oz cottage cheese

juice of 1 lemon

1 tablespoon chopped parsley

salt

freshly ground black pepper

2 eggs, beaten

AMERICAN

1 × 8 inch basic pie dough shell (see
  page 10)

Filling:

3 small kipper fillets

1¼ cups water

2 hard-cooked eggs, chopped

1 cup cottage cheese

juice of 1 lemon

1 tablespoon chopped parsley

salt

freshly ground black pepper

2 eggs, beaten

Simmer the kipper fillets in the water for about 5 to 10 minutes. When cooked, drain, remove any skin and bones, then flake the fish.

In a bowl combine the fish, hard-boiled (hard-cooked) eggs, cottage cheese, lemon juice and parsley.

Add salt and pepper to taste, stir in the beaten eggs and pour into the prepared flan case (pie shell).

Bake in a preheated moderate oven (180°C/350°F, Gas Mark 4) for 25 minutes. Serve hot.

ONION QUICHE (*Photograph: Milk Marketing Board*)

Smoked Haddock Quiche

METRIC/IMPERIAL

1 × 20 cm/8 inch shortcrust pastry
 flan case (see page 10)

Filling:

500 g/1 lb smoked haddock
300 ml/½ pint milk
12 spring onions, chopped
150 ml/¼ pint boiling water
2 hard-boiled eggs, sliced
25 g/1 oz margarine
25 g/1 oz plain flour
50 g/2 oz cheese, grated

AMERICAN

1 × 8 inch basic pie dough shell (see
 page 10)

Filling:

1 lb smoked haddock
1¼ cups milk
12 scallions, chopped
⅔ cup boiling water
2 hard-cooked eggs, sliced
2 tablespoons margarine
¼ cup all-purpose flour
½ cup grated cheese

Place the haddock in a saucepan and add the milk. Poach gently for about
10 minutes. Remove from the heat and drain, reserving the milk.

Flake the haddock, removing any skin and bones, and place in the base
of the prepared flan case (pie shell).

Blanch the spring onions (scallions) in the boiling water, drain and add
to the haddock.

Place the eggs around the edge of the flan (shell).

Melt the margarine in a saucepan, then stir in the flour and cook for
1 minute. Remove from the heat and gradually add the reserved milk.
Heat, stirring, until the sauce thickens. Pour over the haddock and
sprinkle with the cheese.

Bake in a preheated hot oven (220°/425°F, Gas Mark 7) for 15 minutes
or until golden brown. Serve hot.

Cod's Roe and Anchovy Quiche

METRIC/IMPERIAL

1 × 20 cm/8 inch shortcrust pastry flan
  case (see page 10)
Filling:
500 g/1 lb fresh cod's roe
600 ml/1 pint water
1 tablespoon chopped parsley
2 tablespoons white breadcrumbs
2 hard-boiled eggs, chopped
½ teaspoon anchovy paste
1 tablespoon corn oil
1 teaspoon lemon juice
salt
freshly ground black pepper
3 eggs, beaten
75 g/3 oz cheese, grated

AMERICAN

1 × 8 inch basic pie dough shell (see
  page 10)
Filling:
1 lb fresh cod's roe
2½ cups water
1 tablespoon chopped parsley
2 tablespoons white breadcrumbs
2 hard-cooked eggs, chopped
½ teaspoon anchovy paste
1 tablespoon corn oil
1 teaspoon lemon juice
salt
freshly ground black pepper
3 eggs, beaten
¾ cup grated cheese

Poach the cod's roe in the water for 10 to 15 minutes. Drain and then skin
the roe and chop into small pieces. Put the roe into a bowl, add the
parsley, breadcrumbs, hard-boiled (hard-cooked) eggs, anchovy paste, oil
and lemon juice. Mix well together and season with salt and pepper to
taste.

   Place the cod's roe mixture in the prepared flan case (pie shell). Mix the
eggs and grated cheese together and pour over the cod's roe mixture.
Bake in a preheated moderate oven (180°C/350°F, Gas Mark 4) for 30
minutes. Serve hot.

VEGETABLE QUICHES AND FLANS (PIES)

Pepper Quiche

METRIC/IMPERIAL

1 × 20 cm/8 inch shortcrust pastry flan case (see page 10)

Filling:

2 tablespoons oil

25 g/1 oz butter

1 onion, chopped

2 red or green peppers, cored, seeded and sliced

3 eggs

250 ml/8 fl oz milk

salt

freshly ground black pepper

50 g/2 oz fresh breadcrumbs

40 g/1½ oz cheese, grated

AMERICAN

1 × 8 inch basic pie dough shell (see page 10)

Filling:

2 tablespoons oil

2 tablespoons butter

1 onion, chopped

2 red or green peppers, cored, seeded and sliced

3 eggs

1 cup milk

salt

freshly ground black pepper

1 cup fresh breadcrumbs

⅓ cup grated cheese

Heat the oil and butter in a frying pan (skillet) and cook the onion until soft. Add the peppers and continue to cook for 10 minutes. Allow to cool.

Beat together the eggs, milk and salt and pepper to taste. Stir in the breadcrumbs, cheese and peppers. Pour into the prepared flan case (pie shell) and bake in a preheated moderately hot oven (190°C/375°F, Gas Mark 5) for 35 to 40 minutes, until the filling is set and golden. Serve hot.

PEPPER QUICHE *(Photograph: Carmel Produce Information Bureau)*

Provençale Quiche

METRIC/IMPERIAL
1 × 20 cm/8 inch shortcrust pastry flan
  case (see page 10)
Filling:
1 onion, chopped
1 garlic clove, crushed
4 tablespoons oil
1 aubergine, sliced
225 g/8 oz tomatoes, sliced
1 green pepper, cored, seeded and sliced
3 eggs
150 ml/¼ pint milk
salt
freshly ground black pepper
50 g/2 oz cheese, grated
few black olives, stoned

AMERICAN
1 × 8 inch basic pie dough shell (see
  page 10)
Filling:
1 onion, chopped
1 garlic clove, crushed
4 tablespoons oil
1 eggplant, sliced
1 cup sliced tomatoes
1 green pepper, cored, seeded and sliced
3 eggs
⅔ cup milk
salt
freshly ground black pepper
½ cup grated cheese
few ripe olives, pitted

Heat the oil in a large frying pan (skillet) and fry the onion and garlic
until soft. Add the aubergine (eggplant), tomatoes and green pepper and
fry gently for 5 to 10 minutes, stirring occasionally. Remove from the
heat, cool and place the vegetables in the prepared flan case (pie shell).

    Beat together the egg, milk and salt and pepper to taste, and pour over
the aubergine (eggplant) mixture. Sprinkle with the cheese and place the
olives on top. Bake in a preheated moderately hot oven (190°C/375°F,
Gas Mark 5) for 30 to 35 minutes. Serve hot or cold.

Cheesy Vegetable Wheaten Flan (Pie)

METRIC/IMPERIAL
1 × 20 cm/8 inch cheese or wholemeal
  pastry flan case (see page 10)
Filling:
1 egg, beaten
150 ml/¼ pint milk
salt
freshly ground black pepper
350 g/12 oz fresh vegetables, cooked
  (e.g. carrots, peas, leeks)

AMERICAN
1 × 8 inch cheese or wholewheat pie
  shell (see page 10)
Filling:
1 egg, beaten
⅔ cup milk
salt
freshly ground black pepper
2 cups fresh vegetables, cooked (e.g.
  carrots, peas, leeks)

Beat together the egg, milk, salt and pepper. Drain the vegetables well and arrange in the prepared flan case (pie shell). Pour over the egg mixture and place in a preheated moderately hot oven (200°C/400°F, Gas Mark 6) for 30 to 35 minutes until the filling is set and golden. Serve hot or cold.

Courgette (Zucchini) and Cheese Quiche

METRIC/IMPERIAL
1 × 20 cm/8 inch herb pastry flan case
  (see page 10)
Filling:
2 tablespoons oil
1 onion, chopped
500 g/1 lb courgettes, sliced
3 eggs
150 ml/¼ pint milk
salt
freshly ground black pepper
75 g/3 oz cheese, grated

AMERICAN
1 × 8 inch herb dough shell (see
  page 10)
Filling:
2 tablespoons oil
1 onion, chopped
4 cups sliced zucchini
3 eggs
⅔ cup milk
salt
freshly ground black pepper
¾ cup grated cheese

Heat the oil in a frying pan (skillet) and fry the onion until soft. Add the courgettes (zucchini) and cook for 8 to 10 minutes. Place the vegetables in the prepared flan case (pie shell).

Beat together the eggs, milk, and salt and pepper to taste, and pour into the flan case (pie shell). Sprinkle with the cheese and bake in a preheated moderately hot oven (190°C/375°F, Gas Mark 5) for 25 to 30 minutes. Serve hot or cold.

Asparagus Quiche

METRIC/IMPERIAL

1 × 20 cm/8 inch shortcrust pastry flan
  case (see page 10)

Filling:

2 eggs

salt

freshly ground black pepper

150 ml/¼ pint fresh double cream

4 tablespoons milk

1 × 350 g/12 oz can asparagus spears,
  drained

AMERICAN

1 × 8 inch basic pie dough shell (see
  page 10)

Filling:

2 eggs

salt

freshly ground black pepper

⅔ cup heavy cream

4 tablespoons milk

1 × ¾ lb can asparagus spears,
  drained

Beat together the eggs, salt, pepper, cream and milk. Pour into the
prepared flan case (pie shell). Arrange the asparagus spears over the top.

Place in a preheated moderate oven (180°C/350°F, Gas Mark 4) for 20
to 30 minutes until golden. Serve hot or cold.

Sage and Onion Quiche

METRIC/IMPERIAL

1 × 20 cm/8 inch shortcrust or potato
  pastry flan case (see page 10/12)

Filling:

50 g/2 oz butter

2 large onions, sliced

2 eggs

150 ml/¼ pint milk

1 tablespoon chopped sage

1 teaspoon chopped parsley

salt

freshly ground black pepper

50 g/2 oz cheese, grated

tomato slices to garnish

AMERICAN

1 × 8 inch basic pie dough or potato
  shell (see page 10/12)

Filling:

¼ cup butter

2 large onions, sliced

2 eggs

⅔ cup milk

1 tablespoon chopped sage

1 teaspoon chopped parsley

salt

freshly ground black pepper

½ cup grated cheese

tomato slices to garnish

Melt the butter in a frying pan (skillet) and fry the onions until soft.

Beat together the eggs, milk, sage, parsley and salt and pepper to taste.
Place the onions in the prepared flan case (pie shell) and pour over the sage
mixture. Sprinkle with the cheese and bake in a preheated moderately hot
oven (200°C/400°F, Gas Mark 6) for 20 to 25 minutes. Serve hot or cold,
garnished with the tomato slices.

Carrot and Cheese Quiche

METRIC/IMPERIAL
1 × 20 cm/8 inch shortcrust or herb
pastry flan case (see page 10)
Filling:
50 g/2 oz margarine
100 g/4 oz carrot, grated
2 eggs
150 ml/¼ pint single cream
3 tablespoons milk
1 teaspoon chopped chives
salt
freshly ground black pepper
75 g/3 oz Cheddar cheese, grated
parsley sprigs to garnish

AMERICAN
1 × 8 inch basic pie dough or herb pie
shell (see page 10)
Filling:
¼ cup margarine
1 cup grated carrot
2 eggs
⅔ cup light cream
3 tablespoons milk
1 teaspoon chopped chives
salt
freshly ground black pepper
¾ cup grated Cheddar cheese
parsley sprigs to garnish

Melt the margarine in a saucepan and cook the carrot gently for about 5 minutes. Remove from the heat and cool.

Beat together the eggs, cream, milk, chives and salt and pepper to taste. Stir in the carrot and pour into the prepared flan case (pie shell). Sprinkle with the cheese and bake in a preheated moderately hot oven (190°C/ 375°F, Gas Mark 5) for 30 minutes until the filling is set and golden. Serve hot or cold garnished with parsley sprigs.

Cauliflower and Walnut Flan (Pie)

METRIC/IMPERIAL

1 × 20 cm/8 inch cheese pastry flan case (see page 10)

Filling:

1 small cauliflower

50 g/2 oz shelled walnuts

3 eggs

150 ml/¼ pint single cream

salt

freshly ground black pepper

50 g/2 oz Parmesan cheese, grated

Garnish:

tomato slices

few walnut halves

AMERICAN

1 × 8 inch cheese dough shell (see page 10)

Filling:

1 small cauliflower

½ cup shelled walnuts

3 eggs

⅔ cup light cream

salt

freshly ground black pepper

½ cup grated Parmesan cheese

Garnish:

tomato slices

few walnut halves

Break the cauliflower carefully into florets and blanch in salted boiling water for 5 minutes. Drain and place in the prepared flan case (pie shell). Chop the walnuts and sprinkle over the cauliflower.

Beat together the eggs, cream and salt and pepper to taste, then pour over the cauliflower and walnuts. Sprinkle with the cheese and bake in a preheated moderately hot oven (190°C/375°F, Gas Mark 5) for 20 to 25 minutes. Garnish with the tomato slices and walnuts. Serve hot or cold.

Aubergine (Eggplant) and Mushroom Flan (Pie)

METRIC/IMPERIAL

1 × 20 cm/8 inch shortcrust pastry flan
 case (see page 10)

Filling:

2 × 225 g/8 oz aubergines
1 garlic clove, crushed
2 teaspoons oil
2 teaspoons lemon juice
2 eggs
150 ml/¼ pint milk
75 g/3 oz Cheddar cheese, grated
salt
freshly ground black pepper
100 g/4 oz mushrooms

AMERICAN

1 × 8 inch basic pie dough shell (see
 page 10)

Filling:

2 × ½ lb eggplants
1 garlic clove, crushed
2 teaspoons oil
2 teaspoons lemon juice
2 eggs
⅔ cup milk
¾ cup grated Cheddar cheese
salt
freshly ground black pepper
¼ lb mushrooms

Wash the aubergines (eggplants), cut off the stalks and prick in several places. Bake in a preheated moderately hot oven (190°C/375°F, Gas Mark 5) for 40 to 50 minutes until the aubergines (eggplants) are tender and start to collapse. Allow to cool slightly, cut in half and scoop the flesh into a bowl. Add the garlic, oil and lemon juice, then mash until smooth. Spoon into the prepared flan case (pie shell).

Beat together the eggs, milk, cheese and salt and pepper to taste, then pour over the aubergine (eggplant) mixture. Arrange the mushrooms over the top and place in a preheated moderate oven (180°C/350°F, Gas Mark 4) for 30 minutes until golden brown. Serve hot or cold.

AUBERGINE (EGGPLANT) AND MUSHROOM FLAN (PIE)
(Photograph: Carmel Produce Information Bureau)

Spinach and Cottage Cheese Quiche

METRIC/IMPERIAL
1 × 20 cm/8 inch shortcrust pastry flan
   case (see page 10)
Filling:
1 × 225 g/8 oz packet frozen spinach
225 g/8 oz cottage cheese
2 eggs
1 egg yolk
4 tablespoons single cream
1 garlic clove, crushed
salt
freshly ground black pepper
50 g/2 oz Parmesan cheese, grated

AMERICAN
1 × 8 inch basic pie dough shell (see
   page 10)
Filling:
1 × ½ lb package frozen spinach
1 cup cottage cheese
2 eggs
1 egg yolk
4 tablespoons light cream
1 garlic clove, crushed
salt
freshly ground black pepper
½ cup grated Parmesan cheese

Cook the spinach as directed on the packet (package). Remove from the heat, drain and cool.

Beat together the cottage cheese, eggs, egg yolk and cream. Add the garlic, and salt and pepper to taste, then stir in the spinach and mix well. Pour into the prepared flan case (pie shell) and sprinkle with the Parmesan cheese.

Bake in a preheated moderate oven (180°C/350°F, Gas Mark 4) for 30 to 35 minutes until golden. Serve hot or cold.

Marrow (Squash) Niçoise Quiche

METRIC/IMPERIAL

1 × 20 cm/8 inch shortcrust or herb
pastry flan case (see page 10)

Filling:

1 small marrow, peeled, seeded and
sliced

2 tablespoons oil

1 onion, chopped

4 tomatoes, sliced

2 eggs

150 ml/¼ pint milk

150 ml/¼ pint carton natural yogurt

salt

freshly ground black pepper

1 teaspoon thyme

1 teaspoon sage

1 teaspoon fresh parsley, chopped

50 g/2 oz Parmesan cheese, grated

AMERICAN

1 × 8 inch basic pie dough or herb
shell (see page 10)

Filling:

1 small squash, peeled, seeded and
sliced

2 tablespoons oil

1 onion, chopped

4 tomatoes, sliced

2 eggs

⅔ cup milk

⅔ cup unflavored yogurt

salt

freshly ground black pepper

1 teaspoon thyme

1 teaspoon sage

1 teaspoon chopped fresh parsley

½ cup grated Parmesan cheese

Cook the marrow (squash) in boiling, salted water for 5 minutes, then drain. Heat the oil in a frying pan (skillet) and cook the onion and tomato for 5 minutes. Cool slightly and arrange in the prepared flan case (pie shell) with the marrow (squash) on top.

In a bowl beat together the eggs, milk, yogurt, and salt and pepper to taste, thyme, sage and parsley, then pour over the vegetables. Sprinkle with the Parmesan cheese and bake in a preheated moderate oven (180°C/350°F, Gas Mark 4) for 25 to 30 minutes until golden. Serve hot or cold.

MEAT QUICHES AND FLANS (PIES)

Ham, Leek and Olive Flan (Pie)

METRIC/IMPERIAL	AMERICAN
1 × 20 cm/8 inch shortcrust pastry flan case (see page 10)	1 × 8 inch basic pie dough shell (see page 10)
Filling:	**Filling:**
25 g/1 oz butter	2 tablespoons butter
2 leeks, washed, trimmed and cut into rings	2 leeks, washed, trimmed and cut into rings
75 g/3 oz cooked ham, diced	$\frac{1}{3}$ cup chopped cooked ham
6–8 stuffed green olives, halved	6–8 stuffed green olives, halved
2 eggs	2 eggs
150 ml/$\frac{1}{4}$ pint milk	$\frac{2}{3}$ cup milk
salt	salt
freshly ground black pepper	freshly ground black pepper

Melt the butter in a frying pan (skillet) and cook the leeks until softened. Arrange in the prepared flan case (pie shell). Place the ham and olives over the top.

Beat together the eggs, milk, and salt and pepper to taste, then pour over the filling. Place in a preheated moderately hot oven (190°C/375°F, Gas Mark 5) for 35 to 40 minutes until the filling is set and golden. Serve hot or cold.

HAM, LEEK AND OLIVE FLAN (PIE) *(Photograph: Olives from Spain)*

Curried Chicken Quiche

METRIC/IMPERIAL
1 × 20 cm/8 inch shortcrust or curry
  pastry flan case (see page 10)
Filling:
25 g/1 oz margarine
1 onion, sliced
1 dessert apple, peeled, cored and sliced
1 tablespoon curry powder
2 eggs
150 ml/¼ pint milk
salt
175 g/6 oz cooked chicken, chopped
15 g/½ oz raisins

AMERICAN
1 × 8 inch basic pie dough or curry
  shell (see page 10)
Filling:
2 tablespoons margarine
1 onion, sliced
1 dessert apple, peeled, cored and sliced
1 tablespoon curry powder
2 eggs
⅔ cup milk
salt
¾ cup chopped cooked chicken
1–2 tablespoons raisins

Melt the margarine in a frying pan (skillet) and fry the onion and apple for about 5 minutes. Add the curry powder and cook for a further 2 minutes. Remove from the heat and allow to cool.

Beat together the eggs, milk and salt, then stir in the curry mixture.

Arrange the chicken and raisins in the prepared flan case (pie shell), and pour the curry mixture over the top. Bake in a preheated moderately hot oven (200°C/400°F, Gas Mark 6) for 25 to 30 minutes.

Spiced Turkey Flan (Pie)

METRIC/IMPERIAL
1 × 20 cm/8 inch curry pastry flan
  case (see page 10)
Filling:
225 g/8 oz cooked turkey
50 g/2 oz cooked ham
salt
freshly ground black pepper
¼ teaspoon curry powder
¼ teaspoon ground cumin
1 teaspoon made mustard
50 g/2 oz butter
Garnish:
tomato slices

AMERICAN
1 × 8 inch curry dough pie shell (see
  page 10)
Filling:
1 cup chopped cooked turkey
¼ cup chopped cooked ham
salt
freshly ground black pepper
¼ teaspoon curry powder
¼ teaspoon ground cumin
1 teaspoon made mustard
¼ cup butter
Garnish:
tomato slices

Put the turkey and ham through a mincer (grinder). Place in a bowl and add salt and pepper to taste, curry powder, cumin and mustard. Mix well.

Melt the butter in a saucepan, then stir in the meat mixture and mix well together. Spread over the base of the prepared flan case (pie shell) and garnish with the tomatoes. Serve chilled with green salad.

Ham and Egg Flan (Pie)

METRIC/IMPERIAL

1 × 20 cm/8 inch shortcrust or herb
  pastry flan case (see page 10)
Filling:
50 g/2 oz margarine
1 onion, chopped
50 g/2 oz plain flour
300 ml/½ pint milk
100 g/4 oz cooked ham, chopped
3 hard-boiled eggs, sliced
salt and pepper
Garnish:
1 tablespoon chopped parsley
1 × 25 g/1 oz packet cheese-flavoured
  potato crisps, crushed
1 tomato, sliced, to garnish

AMERICAN

1 × 8 inch basic pie dough or herb
  shell (see page 10)
Filling:
¼ cup margarine
1 onion, chopped
½ cup all-purpose flour
1¼ cups milk
½ cup chopped cooked ham
3 hard-cooked eggs, sliced
salt and pepper
Garnish:
1 tablespoon chopped parsley
3 tablespoons crushed cheese-flavored
  potato chips
1 tomato, sliced, to garnish

Melt the margarine in a saucepan and fry the onion until soft. Stir in the
flour and cook for 1 minute. Remove from the heat and gradually blend
in the milk. Heat, stirring until the sauce thickens. Cool slightly then add
the chopped ham, eggs and salt and pepper to taste. Pour into the
prepared flan case (pie shell) and chill in the refrigerator.

Before serving sprinkle parsley and potato crisps (chips) over the flan
and arrange the sliced tomato in the centre.

Ham Sausage and Artichoke Flan (Pie)

METRIC/IMPERIAL

1 × 20 cm/8 inch shortcrust pastry flan
  case (see page 10)

Filling:

225 g/8 oz Jerusalem artichokes,
  peeled and sliced

300 ml/½ pint milk

25 g/1 oz butter

25 g/1 oz plain flour

nutmeg

salt

freshly ground black pepper

100 g/4 oz cheese, grated

100 g/4 oz ham sausage, sliced

AMERICAN

1 × 8 inch basic pie dough shell (see
  page 10)

Filling:

1⅓ cups Jerusalem artichokes, peeled
  and sliced

1¼ cups milk

2 tablespoons butter

¼ cup all-purpose flour

nutmeg

salt

freshly ground black pepper

1 cup grated cheese

½ cup ham sausage, sliced

Place the artichokes and milk in a saucepan. Bring to the boil, lower the
heat and simmer for 5 minutes. Drain and reserve the milk.

Rinse the pan and melt the butter. Stir in the flour and cook, stirring,
for 1 minute. Remove from the heat and gradually blend in the reserved
milk. Return to the heat, and cook, stirring, until the sauce thickens, stir
in the cheese then add nutmeg, salt and pepper to taste.

Arrange the artichokes and ham sausage in the prepared flan case (pie
shell) and pour the sauce over. Place in a preheated moderately hot oven
(190°C/375°F, Gas Mark 5) for 25 to 30 minutes. Serve hot.

HAM SAUSAGE AND ARTICHOKE FLAN (PIE) *(Photograph:
Mattesons)*

Kidney and Green Pepper Quiche

METRIC/IMPERIAL

1 × 20 cm/8 inch shortcrust or herb
  pastry flan case (see page 10)
Filling:
25 g/1 oz butter
1 onion, chopped
6 lambs' kidneys, cored and sliced
1 green pepper, cored, seeded and
  chopped
3 eggs
3 tablespoons milk
salt
freshly ground black pepper

AMERICAN

1 × 8 inch basic pie dough or herb
  shell (see page 10)
Filling:
2 tablespoons butter
1 onion, chopped
6 lambs' kidneys, cored and sliced
1 green pepper, cored, seeded and
  chopped
3 eggs
3 tablespoons milk
salt
freshly ground black pepper

Melt the butter in a frying pan (skillet) and fry the onion until soft. Add
the kidneys and green pepper and cook gently for 5 minutes. Remove
from the heat. Beat together the eggs and milk and season with salt and
pepper.

Spread the kidney and green pepper mixture over the base of the
prepared flan case (pie shell) and pour over the egg mixture. Bake in a
preheated moderate oven (180°C/350°F, Gas Mark 4) for 35 to 40 minutes.
Serve hot.

Pork and Spinach Quiche

METRIC/IMPERIAL

1 × 20 cm/8 inch shortcrust or cheese
  pastry flan case (see page 10)

Filling:
1 × 225 g/8 oz packet frozen spinach
100 g/4 oz butter
2 tablespoons oil
1 onion, chopped
100 g/4 oz minced beef
175 g/6 oz minced pork
salt
freshly ground black pepper
1 tablespoon plain flour
50 g/2 oz Parmesan cheese, grated
2 tablespoons double cream

Garnish:
tomato slices
parsley

AMERICAN

1 × 8 inch basic pie dough or cheese
  shell (see page 10)

Filling:
1 × ½ lb package frozen spinach
½ cup butter
2 tablespoons oil
1 onion, chopped
½ cup ground beef
¾ cup ground pork
salt
freshly ground black pepper
1 tablespoon all-purpose flour
½ cup grated Parmesan cheese
2 tablespoons heavy cream

Garnish:
tomato slices
parsley

Cook the frozen spinach as directed on the packet (package).

Melt 50 g/2 oz (¼ cup) butter and the oil in a frying pan (skillet), and fry the onion until soft.

Add the beef and pork and cook over a gentle heat, mixing thoroughly, for 15 to 20 minutes. Add salt and pepper to taste, the flour and Parmesan cheese and mix well. Continue cooking for another 5 minutes, stirring well. Remove from the heat and allow to cool.

Place the spinach in a saucepan with the remaining 50 g/2 oz (¼ cup) butter and fry for 5 minutes. Stir in the cream and mix well.

Place half the meat mixture in the prepared flan case (pie shell), spread the spinach and cream on top and cover with the remaining meat mixture. Bake in a preheated moderately hot oven (200°C/400°F, Gas Mark 6) for 35 to 40 minutes. Garnish with the tomato and parsley and serve hot.

Spanish Flan (Pie)

METRIC/IMPERIAL

1 × 20 cm/8 inch shortcrust pastry flan
  case (see page 10)
Filling:
100 g/4 oz streaky bacon, derinded
  and chopped
75 g/3 oz Lancashire cheese, crumbled
12 stuffed green olives, halved
2 eggs, beaten
150 ml/¼ pint single cream
salt
freshly ground black pepper

AMERICAN

1 × 8 inch basic pie dough shell (see
  page 10)
Filling:
½ cup chopped fatty bacon,
  derinded
¾ cup crumbled Lancashire cheese
12 stuffed green olives, halved
2 eggs, beaten
⅔ cup light cream
salt
freshly ground black pepper

Fry the bacon in its own fat in a frying pan (skillet) until almost crisp.
Drain on kitchen paper (towels) and place in the prepared flan case (pie
shell). Cover with the cheese and olives.

Beat together the eggs, cream, and salt and pepper to taste, and pour
over the filling. Place in a preheated moderate oven (180°C/350°F, Gas
Mark 4) for 25 to 30 minutes until the filling is set and golden. Serve hot
or cold.

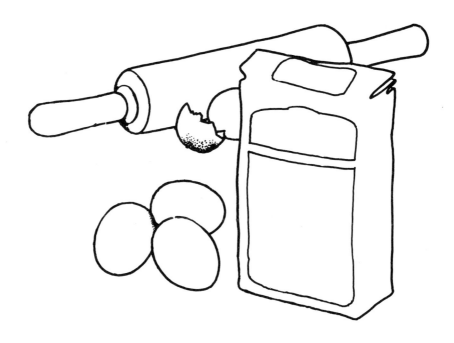

SPANISH FLAN (PIE) *(Photograph: Olives from Spain)*

Broad Bean and Ham Flan (Pie)

METRIC/IMPERIAL
1 × 20 cm/8 inch shortcrust pastry flan case (see page 10)
Filling:
40 g/1½ oz butter
25 g/1 oz plain flour
300 ml/½ pint milk
1 × 275 g/10 oz can broad beans
2 tablespoons chopped parsley
225 g/8 oz cooked ham, diced
salt
freshly ground black pepper

AMERICAN
1 × 8 inch basic pie dough shell (see page 10)
Filling:
3 tablespoons butter
¼ cup all-purpose flour
1¼ cups milk
1 × 10 oz can lima beans
2 tablespoons chopped parsley
1 cup diced cooked ham
salt
freshly ground black pepper

Melt the butter in a saucepan, then stir in the flour and cook for 1 minute. Remove from the heat and gradually blend in the milk. Return to the heat and cook, stirring, until the sauce thickens. Stir in the beans, parsley and meat, then add salt and pepper to taste. Pour into the prepared flan case (pie shell) and serve immediately.

Bacon Curry and Yogurt Quiche

METRIC/IMPERIAL
1 × 20 cm/8 inch shortcrust pastry flan case (see page 10)
Filling:
50 g/2 oz margarine
175 g/6 oz streaky bacon, chopped
100 g/4 oz celery, chopped
1 teaspoon curry powder
150 ml/¼ pint carton natural yogurt
3 eggs
2 tomatoes, sliced, to garnish

AMERICAN
1 × 8 inch basic pie dough shell (see page 10)
Filling:
¼ cup margarine
9 fatty bacon slices, chopped
1 cup chopped celery
1 teaspoon curry powder
⅔ cup unflavored yogurt
3 eggs
2 tomatoes, sliced, to garnish

Melt the margarine in a frying pan (skillet) and fry the bacon and celery for 3 minutes; add the curry powder and fry for a further 2 minutes.

Beat together the yogurt and eggs, add to the bacon and celery, mix well and pour into the prepared flan case (pie shell). Bake in a preheated moderate oven (180°C/350°F, Gas Mark 4) for 25 minutes. Garnish with the tomato slices and serve hot.

Bacon and Liver Sausage Flan (Pie)

METRIC/IMPERIAL

1 × 20 cm/8 inch shortcrust or cheese pastry flan case (see page 10)

Filling:
100 g/4 oz liver sausage, thinly sliced
50 g/2 oz margarine
50 g/2 oz streaky bacon, derinded and chopped
50 g/2 oz plain flour
150 ml/¼ pint milk
1 tablespoon chopped parsley
salt and pepper
1 hard-boiled egg, sliced

AMERICAN

1 × 8 inch basic pie dough or cheese shell (see page 10)

Filling:
½ cup thinly sliced liver sausage
¼ cup margarine
3 fatty bacon slices, derinded and chopped
½ cup all-purpose flour
⅔ cup milk
1 tablespoon chopped parsley
salt and pepper
1 hard-cooked egg, sliced

Place the liver sausage in the prepared flan case (pie shell).

Fry the bacon in its own fat in a frying pan (skillet) until soft. Remove from the heat and sprinkle over the liver sausage.

Melt the margarine in a saucepan then stir in the flour and cook, stirring continuously, for 1 minute. Remove from the heat and gradually blend in the milk, stirring until the sauce thickens. Stir in the parsley and add salt and pepper to taste. Pour over the liver sausage and bacon, and cook in a preheated moderately hot oven (190°C/375°F, Gas Mark 5) for 25 minutes.

Garnish with the egg and serve hot.

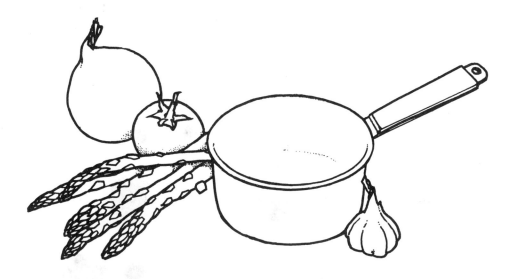

FISH QUICHES AND FLANS (PIES)

Smoked Mackerel Flans (Pies)

METRIC/IMPERIAL

4 × 10 cm/4 inch shortcrust pastry
  flan cases (made from 175 g/6 oz
  flour – see page 10)
Filling:
1 × 200 g/7 oz can smoked mackerel
  fillets
100 g/4 oz cooked rice
2 hard-boiled eggs, chopped
50 g/2 oz cucumber, diced
2 tablespoons salad cream
2 teaspoons chopped chives
salt
freshly ground black pepper
Garnish:
lemon wedges
parsley

AMERICAN

4 × 4 inch basic pie dough shells
  (made from 1½ cups flour – see
  page 10)
Filling:
1 × 7 oz can smoked mackerel
  fillets
½ cup cooked rice
2 hard-cooked eggs, chopped
½ cup diced cucumber
2 tablespoons salad cream
2 teaspoons chopped chives
salt
freshly ground black pepper
Garnish:
lemon wedges
parsley

Drain the mackerel fillets, remove the skin and flake the fish.
   Mix together the remaining filling ingredients and add the mackerel.
Divide the mixture between the prepared flan cases (pie shells) and
garnish with lemon wedges and parsley. Serve lightly chilled.

SMOKED MACKEREL FLANS (PIES) *(Photograph: Canned Food
Advisory Service)*

Cod and Leek Quiche

METRIC/IMPERIAL

1 × 20 cm/8 inch shortcrust or cheese
  pastry flan case (see page 10)
Filling:
25 g/1 oz butter
225 g/8 oz leeks, sliced
225 g/8 oz cod
300 ml/½ pint milk
50 g/2 oz margarine
50 g/2 oz plain flour
salt and pepper
1 tablespoon chopped parsley

AMERICAN

1 × 8 inch basic pie dough or cheese
  shell (see page 10)
Filling:
2 tablespoons butter
2 cups chopped leeks
½ lb cod
1¼ cups milk
¼ cup margarine
½ cup all-purpose flour
salt and pepper
1 tablespoon chopped parsley

Melt the butter in a frying pan (skillet) and fry the leeks for about 5
minutes. Place the cod and milk in a saucepan and poach for about 10
minutes. Remove from the heat and drain, reserving the milk. Flake the
cod, removing any skin and bone.

In another saucepan melt the margarine then stir in the flour and cook
for 1 minute, stirring continuously. Remove from the heat and gradually
add the reserved milk. Heat, stirring, until the sauce thickens.

Combine the leeks, cod, salt and pepper to taste, and parsley with the
sauce and pour into the prepared flan case (pie shell). Bake in a preheated
moderately hot oven (200°C/400°F, Gas Mark 6) for 30 minutes until
golden. Serve hot.

Tunisian Fish Flan (Pie)

METRIC/IMPERIAL

1 × 20 cm/8 inch shortcrust or cheese
  pastry flan case (see page 10)
Filling:
50 g/2 oz butter
1 onion, chopped
50 g/2 oz flour
300 ml/½ pint milk
salt and pepper
pinch of nutmeg
2 hard-boiled eggs, sliced
2 tomatoes, sliced
350 g/12 oz cooked white fish,
  skinned, flaked and boned
100 g/4 oz cheese, grated

AMERICAN

1 × 8 inch basic pie dough or cheese
  shell (see page 10)
Filling:
¼ cup butter
1 onion, chopped
½ cup flour
1¼ cups milk
salt and pepper
pinch of nutmeg
2 hard-cooked eggs, sliced
2 tomatoes, sliced
¾ lb cooked white fish, skinned,
  flaked and boned
1 cup grated cheese

Melt the butter in a saucepan and fry the onion until soft. Stir in the flour and cook for 1 minute. Remove from the heat and gradually add the milk. Heat, stirring, until the sauce thickens. Add the salt, pepper and nutmeg to taste.

Place the eggs and tomatoes over the base of the prepared flan case (pie shell) and cover with the flaked fish. Pour the sauce over and sprinkle with the cheese. Bake in a preheated moderately hot oven (190°C/375°F, Gas Mark 5) for 35 to 40 minutes until golden. Serve hot.

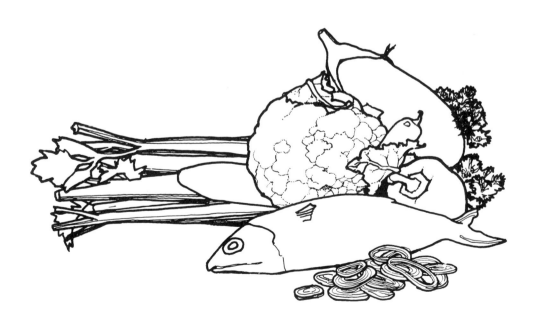

Kipper Cream Flan (Pie)

METRIC/IMPERIAL	AMERICAN
1 × 20 cm/8 inch cheese and oat flan case (see page 12)	1 × 8 inch cheese and oat pie shell (see page 12)
Filling:	**Filling:**
100 g/4 oz cucumber, diced	1 cup diced cucumber
2 celery sticks, chopped	2 celery sticks
4 spring onions, chopped	4 scallions, chopped
150 ml/¼ pint soured cream	⅔ cup sour cream
1 teaspoon lemon juice	1 teaspoon lemon juice
salt	salt
freshly ground black pepper	freshly ground black pepper
1 × 200 g/7 oz can kipper fillets, drained	1 × 7 oz can kipper fillets, drained
Garnish:	**Garnish:**
2 hard-boiled eggs, quartered	2 hard-cooked eggs, quartered
parsley	parsley

Mix together the cucumber, celery, spring onions (scallions), soured (sour) cream, lemon juice and salt and pepper to taste. Flake the kipper fillets removing any skin or bones and fold into the mixture.

Spoon into the prepared flan case (pie shell) and garnish with the hard-boiled (hard-cooked) eggs and parsley.

Crab Quiche

METRIC/IMPERIAL	AMERICAN
1 × 20 cm/8 inch shortcrust pastry flan case (see page 10)	1 × 8 inch basic pie dough shell (see page 10)
Filling:	**Filling:**
225 g/8 oz crab meat	½ lb crab meat
3 eggs	3 eggs
450 ml/¾ pint double cream	2 cups heavy cream
salt and pepper	salt and pepper

Break up the crab meat with a fork. Place the eggs and cream in a bowl and beat together, then stir in the crab meat and salt and pepper to taste, mixing until well blended. Place in the prepared flan case (pie shell) and bake in a preheated moderately hot oven (190°C/375°F, Gas Mark 5) for 35 to 40 minutes until golden. Serve immediately.

From top: INDIVIDUAL SEAFARERS QUICHES *(page 62),*
KIPPER CREAM FLAN (PIE) and ASPARAGUS BARQUETTES
(page 22) (Photograph: John West Foods)

Crab and Wine Quiche

METRIC/IMPERIAL
1 × 20 cm/8 inch shortcrust pastry flan
  case (see page 10)
Filling:
225 g/8 oz crab meat, flaked
150 ml/¼ pint dry white wine
150 ml/¼ pint double cream
2 eggs
1 egg yolk
50 g/2 oz Parmesan cheese, grated
salt and pepper

AMERICAN
1 × 8 inch basic pie dough shell (see
  page 10)
Filling:
½ lb crab meat, flaked
⅔ cup dry white wine
⅔ cup heavy cream
2 eggs
1 egg yolk
½ cup grated Parmesan cheese
salt and pepper

Place the crab meat in a saucepan and add the white wine. Poach gently for about 5 minutes then remove from the heat.

Beat together the cream, eggs and egg yolk in a bowl. Stir in the crab and wine mixture and mix well. Add the Parmesan cheese and salt and pepper to taste, then pour into the prepared flan case (pie shell). Bake in a preheated moderately hot oven (190°C/375°F, Gas Mark 5) for 35 to 40 minutes until golden. Serve at once.

Curried Prawn (Shrimp) Quiche

METRIC/IMPERIAL
1 × 20 cm/8 inch shortcrust or curry
  pastry flan case (see page 10)
Filling:
50 g/2 oz butter
1 onion, chopped
1 tablespoon curry powder
2 eggs, beaten
150 ml/¼ pint milk
salt
275 g/10 oz shelled prawns

AMERICAN
1 × 8 inch basic pie dough or curry
  shell (see page 10)
Filling:
¼ cup butter
1 onion, chopped
1 tablespoon curry powder
2 eggs, beaten
⅔ cup milk
salt
1¾ cups shelled shrimp

Melt the butter in a saucepan and fry the onion for about 5 minutes, until soft. Add the curry powder and cook for a further 2 minutes. Remove from the heat and cool.

Blend together the eggs and milk and add salt to taste. Stir in the curry mixture until well blended.

Arrange the prawns (shrimp) in the base of the prepared flan case (pie shell) then pour over the curry mixture. Bake in a preheated moderately hot oven (190°C/375°F, Gas Mark 5) for 25 to 30 minutes. Serve hot.

Luxury Seafood Quiche

METRIC/IMPERIAL

*1 × 20 cm/8 inch shortcrust or cheese
 pastry case (see page 10)*
Filling:
25 g/1 oz butter
*1 green pepper, cored, seeded and
 sliced*
50 g/2 oz button mushrooms, sliced
3 eggs
150 ml/¼ pint single cream
salt
freshly ground black pepper
1 garlic clove, crushed
*1 × 115 g/4½ oz can mackerel fillets,
 drained*
*1 × 90 g/3½ oz can smoked mussels,
 drained*
75 g/3 oz shelled prawns

AMERICAN

*1 × 8 inch basic pie dough or cheese
 shell (see page 10)*
Filling:
2 tablespoons butter
*1 green pepper, cored, seeded and
 sliced*
½ cup sliced button mushrooms
3 eggs
⅔ cup light cream
salt
freshly ground black pepper
1 garlic clove, crushed
*1 × 4½ oz can mackerel fillets,
 drained*
*1 × 3½ oz can smoked mussels,
 drained*
½ cup shelled shrimp

Melt the butter in a frying pan (skillet) and fry the pepper and mushrooms
until soft. Beat together the eggs, cream and salt and pepper to taste.

Remove any skin and bones from the mackerel and flake the fish.
Arrange in the prepared flan case (pie shell) with the mussels, prawns
(shrimp) and vegetables. Pour the egg mixture over and bake in a
preheated moderately hot oven (200°C/400°F, Gas Mark 6) for 25
minutes until set and golden. Serve hot.

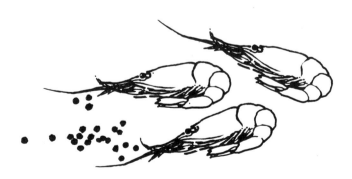

Salmon and Mushroom Quiche

METRIC/IMPERIAL

1 × 20 cm/8 inch shortcrust pastry flan
  case (see page 10)

Filling:

25 g/1 oz butter
50 g/2 oz button mushrooms, sliced
1 small onion, finely chopped
1 × 215 g/7½ oz can pink salmon
1 egg
150 ml/¼ pint milk
2 teaspoons horseradish sauce
salt
freshly ground black pepper
50 g/2 oz Edam cheese, grated

AMERICAN

1 × 8 inch basic pie dough shell (see
  page 10)

Filling:

2 tablespoons butter
½ cup sliced button mushrooms
1 small onion, finely chopped
1 × 7½ oz can pink salmon
1 egg
⅔ cup milk
2 teaspoons horseradish sauce
salt
freshly ground black pepper
½ cup grated Edam cheese

Melt the butter in a frying pan (skillet) and fry the mushrooms and onion until soft. Place in the prepared flan case (pie shell). Drain the salmon, remove any skin and bones, then flake the fish. Arrange over the mushrooms and onion.

Beat together the egg, milk, horseradish sauce, salt and pepper to taste, and the cheese. Pour over the salmon and bake in a preheated moderately hot oven (200°C/400°F, Gas Mark 6) for 25 to 30 minutes until just set and golden. Serve hot or cold.

From top, clockwise: PISSALADIERE *(page 63)*, LUXURY SEAFOOD QUICHE *(page 59)* and SALMON AND MUSHROOM QUICHE
(Photograph: John West Foods)

Individual Seafood Quiches

METRIC/IMPERIAL

6 × 10 cm/4 inch shortcrust pastry flan
 cases (made from 275 g/10 oz flour –
 see page 10)

Filling:

15 g/½ oz butter

1 onion, finely chopped

1 × 200 g/7 oz can tuna, drained

1 × 225 g/8 oz can tomatoes, drained

9 tablespoons sweetcorn kernels

2 eggs

150 ml/¼ pint single cream

salt

freshly ground black pepper

watercress to garnish

AMERICAN

6 × 4 inch basic pie dough shells
 (made from 2½ cups flour – see
 page 10)

Filling:

1 tablespoon butter

1 onion, finely chopped

1 × 7 oz can tuna, drained

1 × 8 oz can tomatoes, drained

9 tablespoons sweetcorn kernels

2 eggs

⅔ cup light cream

salt

freshly ground black pepper

watercress to garnish

Melt the butter in a saucepan and fry the onion until soft. Sprinkle a little into each prepared flan case (pie shell). Flake the tuna and place over the top. Divide the tomatoes and sweetcorn between the flans (shells).

Beat together the eggs, cream and salt and pepper to taste, then pour over the filling. Bake in a preheated moderately hot oven (200°C/400°F, Gas Mark 6) for 25 minutes until just set and golden. Serve hot or cold garnished with watercress.

Pissaladière

METRIC/IMPERIAL

1 × 20 cm/8 inch herb pastry case (or long rectangular case) (see page 10)
Filling:
2 tablespoons olive oil
500 g/1 lb onions, sliced
1 × 400 g/14 oz can tomatoes
1 garlic clove, crushed
1 bay leaf
salt
freshly ground black pepper
1 × 50 g/2 oz can anchovy fillets, drained
few black olives
oil, for brushing

AMERICAN

1 × 8 inch herb dough shell (or long rectangular shell) (see page 10)
Filling:
2 tablespoons olive oil
4 cups sliced onion
1 × 14 oz can tomatoes
1 garlic clove, crushed
1 bay leaf
salt
freshly ground black pepper
1 × 2 oz can anchovy fillets, drained
few ripe olives
oil, for brushing

Heat the oil in a saucepan and fry the onions until soft. Add the tomatoes with their juice, garlic, bay leaf and salt and pepper to taste. Bring to the boil, then simmer until the onions are cooked and the liquid has reduced by one third. Remove the bay leaf and spread the mixture over the base of the prepared pastry case (pie shell).

Cut the anchovies in half lengthwise and arrange in a lattice over the filling. Cut the olives in half, remove the stones (seeds) and arrange in the spaces between the anchovies.

Brush the surface with oil and bake in a preheated moderately hot oven (200°C/400°F, Gas Mark 6) for 15 to 20 minutes. Serve hot or cold.

SWEET QUICHES AND FLANS (PIES)

Sugar Plum Flan (Pie)

METRIC/IMPERIAL
1 × 20 cm/8 inch French flan pastry
  case (see page 11)
Filling:
3 egg yolks
15 g/½ oz granulated sugar
300 ml/½ pint natural yogurt
½ teaspoon cinnamon
500 g/1 lb dessert plums
25 g/1 oz blanched almonds
40 g/1½ oz demerara sugar

AMERICAN
1 × 8 inch French pie dough shell
  (see page 11)
Filling:
3 eggs yolks
1 tablespoon sugar
1¼ cups unflavored yogurt
½ teaspoon cinnamon
4 cups dessert plums
¼ cup blanched almonds
¼ cup brown sugar

Beat together the egg yolks, sugar, yogurt and cinnamon, then pour into the prepared flan case (pie shell).

Cut the plums in half and remove the stones (seeds), then arrange, cut side up, in the yogurt custard.

Place in a preheated moderately hot oven (200°C/400°F, Gas Mark 6) for 35 to 40 minutes until the filling is set. Remove from the oven and place an almond in the centre of each plum. Sprinkle with the demerara (brown) sugar and place under a hot grill until golden brown. Serve hot or warm.

SUGAR PLUM FLAN (PIE) *(Photograph: Milk Marketing Board)*

Strawberry Flan (Pie)

METRIC/IMPERIAL

1 × 20 cm/8 inch sponge flan case (see
  page 15)
Filling:
350 g/12 oz strawberries
225 g/8 oz redcurrant jelly
To decorate:
150 ml/¼ pint double cream, whipped
grated rind of 1 orange

AMERICAN

1 × 8 inch sponge shell (see page
  15)
Filling:
2½ cups strawberries
¾ cup redcurrant jelly
To decorate:
⅔ cup heavy cream, whipped
grated rind of 1 orange

Hull and wipe the strawberries, then place in the prepared flan case (pie shell).

Place the redcurrant jelly in a saucepan and heat until it comes to the boil. Continue cooking until it becomes clear. Cool slightly, then spoon the glaze over the strawberries. Leave to set.

When set and cold decorate the flan (pie) with the whipped cream and grated orange rind. Serve chilled.

Lemon Ginger Flan (Pie)

METRIC/IMPERIAL

1 × 20 cm/8 inch ginger or lemon
  biscuit flan case (see page 14)
Filling:
150 ml/¼ pint double cream
1 × 375 g/13 oz can sweetened
  condensed milk
grated rind of 2 lemons
juice of 3 lemons
chopped preserved ginger to decorate

AMERICAN

1 × 8 inch ginger or lemon cracker pie
  shell (see page 14)
Filling:
⅔ cup heavy cream
1 × 13 oz can sweetened condensed
  milk
grated rind of 2 lemons
juice of 3 lemons
chopped preserved ginger to decorate

Place the cream in a bowl and whip until thick. Blend in the condensed milk, lemon rind and juice. Spoon into the prepared flan case (pie shell) and decorate with the ginger. Chill thoroughly before serving.

Note: The cream mixture will thicken during chilling in the refrigerator.

Apple and Hazelnut Flan (Pie)

METRIC/IMPERIAL

1 × 20 cm/8 inch French flan pastry
  case (see page 11)
Filling:
350 g/12 oz cooking apples
25 g/1 oz sugar
25 g/1 oz hazelnuts, chopped
2 red skinned dessert apples
2 tablespoons apricot jam
1 tablespoon water
150 ml/¼ pint double cream, whipped,
  to decorate

AMERICAN

1 × 8 inch French pie dough shell (see
  page 11)
Filling:
¾ lb cooking apples
2 tablespoons sugar
¼ cup chopped hazelnuts
2 red skinned dessert apples
2 tablespoons apricot jam
1 tablespoon water
⅔ cup heavy cream, whipped,
  to decorate

Peel, core and chop the apples, then place in a saucepan with the sugar. Cook over a low heat for 10 minutes or until the apples are soft and pulpy. Stir in the hazelnuts and leave to cool.

Spoon the mixture into the prepared flan case (pie shell). Remove the cores from the dessert apples and cut into thin slices. Arrange over the apple mixture.

Place the jam and water in a saucepan and heat to make a syrup. Brush over the apple slices, then place the flan (shell) in a preheated moderately hot oven (200°C/400°F, Gas Mark 6) for 15 minutes. Serve warm or cold decorated with the cream and a few hazelnuts.

Mincemeat and Pineapple Flan (Pie)

METRIC/IMPERIAL

1 × 20 cm/8 inch shortcrust pastry flan
  case (see page 10)
Filling:
1 × 500 g/1 lb jar mincemeat
1 × 375 g/13 oz can crushed
  pineapple, drained
1 teaspoon mixed spice
150 ml/¼ pint double cream,
  whipped, to decorate

AMERICAN

1 × 8 inch basic pie dough shell (see
  page 10)
Filling:
1 × 1 lb jar mincemeat
1 × 13 oz can crushed pineapple,
  drained
1 teaspoon mixed spice
⅔ cup heavy cream, whipped, to
  decorate

Mix together the mincemeat, crushed pineapple and mixed spice. Spread the mixture in the bottom of the prepared flan case (pie shell) and bake in a preheated moderately hot oven (190°C/375°F, Gas Mark 5) for 20 to 25 minutes. Leave until completely cold before decorating with the cream.

Orange Quiche

METRIC/IMPERIAL

1 × 20 cm/8 inch shortcrust pastry flan case (see page 10)

Filling:

1 × 300 g/11 oz can mandarin oranges, drained

2 eggs

150 ml/¼ pint single cream

2 tablespoons orange syrup

AMERICAN

1 × 8 inch basic pie dough shell (see page 10)

Filling:

1 × 11 oz can mandarin oranges, drained

2 eggs

⅔ cup light cream

2 tablespoons orange syrup

Arrange the mandarins in the base of the prepared flan case (pie shell).

Beat the eggs and add the cream and orange syrup. Pour over the oranges and place in a preheated moderately hot oven (190°C/375°F, Gas Mark 5) for 30 minutes or until the filling is set. Serve cold with cream.

Apricot and Almond Flan (Pie)

METRIC/IMPERIAL

1 × 20 cm/8 inch French pastry flan case (see page 11)

Filling:

300 ml/½ pint milk

25 g/1 oz caster sugar

25 g/1 oz cornflour

2 egg yolks

¼ teaspoon almond essence

To decorate:

1 × 400 g/14 oz can apricot halves

1 teaspoon arrowroot

blanched whole almonds, toasted

AMERICAN

1 × 8 inch French pie dough shell (see page 11)

Filling:

1¼ cups milk

2 tablespoons sugar

¼ cup cornstarch

2 egg yolks

¼ teaspoon almond extract

To decorate:

1 × 14 oz can apricot halves

1 teaspoon arrowroot flour

blanched whole almonds, toasted

Heat the milk and sugar in a saucepan. Mix together the cornflour (cornstarch) and egg yolks, then pour the hot milk over and stir well. Strain back into the pan and heat, stirring continuously until the mixture thickens. Remove from the heat, stir in the almond essence (extract) and leave to cool.

Spread the custard over the base of the prepared pastry case (pie shell). Drain the apricots, reserving the juice, and arrange the fruit hollow side up on the custard.

Blend the arrowroot (arrowroot flour) with the apricot juice and heat, stirring until the mixture thickens and clears. Cool slightly. Place an almond in each apricot hollow and brush over the fruit with the glaze. Serve chilled.

ORANGE QUICHE (Photograph: Delrosa)

Blackcurrant Flan (Pie)

METRIC/IMPERIAL

1 × 20 cm/8 inch shortbread flan case
(see page 15)

Filling:

40 g/1½ oz cornflour

50 g/2 oz caster sugar

1 egg, beaten

450 ml/¾ pint milk

150 ml/¼ pint double cream

2 tablespoons Kirsch (optional)

Topping:

225 g/8 oz blackcurrants, stalks
removed, and washed

2 tablespoons sugar

2 teaspoons arrowroot

2 tablespoons water

AMERICAN

1 × 8 inch shortbread shell (see
page 15)

Filling:

¼ cup + 2 tablespoons cornstarch

¼ cup sugar

1 egg, beaten

2 cups milk

⅔ cup heavy cream

2 tablespoons Kirsch (optional)

Topping:

2 cups blackcurrants, stalks removed,
and washed

2 tablespoons sugar

2 teaspoons arrowroot flour

2 tablespoons water

Blend the cornflour (cornstarch) with the sugar, egg and 3 tablespoons of the milk.

Heat the remaining milk until almost boiling then pour onto the cornflour (cornstarch) mixture and stir well. Return to the saucepan and heat, stirring, until the mixture thickens. Continue to cook for 1 minute. Pour into a bowl and leave to cool.

Whip the cream with the Kirsch, if used, until thick. Whisk or beat the cooled custard until smooth, then fold in the cream. Spoon into the prepared flan case (pie shell).

To make the topping, place the blackcurrants in a saucepan with the sugar and cook gently for 10 minutes until the fruit is soft. Remove from the heat and strain the blackcurrant juice into a clean saucepan. Blend the arrowroot (arrowroot flour) with the water and stir into the blackcurrant juice. Heat, stirring continuously, until the mixture thickens and clears. Simmer for 2 minutes, then stir in the blackcurrants. Leave to cool before spreading over the custard in the flan (pie shell). Serve chilled.

Cherry Praline Flan (Pie)

METRIC/IMPERIAL

1 × 20 cm/8 inch almond pastry case
  (see page 11)

Filling:

50 g/2 oz shelled almonds
50 g/2 oz caster sugar
1 tablespoon custard powder
150 ml/¼ pint milk
150 ml/¼ pint double cream, whipped

Topping:

1 × 425 g/15 oz can black cherries,
  drained
120 ml/4 fl oz red wine
3 tablespoons redcurrant jelly
grated rind and juice of 1 orange

AMERICAN

1 × 8 inch almond pie dough shell
  (see page 11)

Filling:

½ cup shelled almonds
¼ cup sugar
1 tablespoon vanilla cornstarch
⅔ cup milk
⅔ cup heavy cream, whipped

Topping:

1 × 15 oz can bing cherries,
  drained
½ cup red wine
3 tablespoons redcurrant jelly
grated rind and juice of 1 orange

Place the almonds and sugar in a saucepan and heat gently until the sugar is a liquid caramel. Stir carefully to brown the nuts on all sides. Remove from the heat and pour onto an oiled baking sheet and leave until set. When hard, crush the praline with a rolling pin.

Blend the custard powder (vanilla cornstarch) with a little of the milk. Heat the remaining milk in a saucepan until almost boiling then pour onto custard (vanilla cornstarch). Stir well and return to the pan. Heat, stirring, until the custard thickens, then continue to cook for 1 minute. Pour into a bowl and leave to cool. Beat until smooth, then fold in the cream and praline. Spoon into the prepared flan case (pie shell).

Place the wine in a saucepan and boil until reduced by half. Stir in the redcurrant jelly, orange rind and juice, then heat gently until the jelly has melted. Add most of the cherries and leave to cool.

Spread the fruit over the praline custard and decorate with the remaining cherries. Serve chilled.

Butterscotch Flan (Pie)

METRIC/IMPERIAL
1 × 20 cm/8 inch cornflake crust case
 (see page 12)
Filling:
100 g/4 oz soft brown sugar
50 g/2 oz plain flour
450 ml/¾ pint milk
2 egg yolks
25 g/1 oz butter
½ teaspoon vanilla essence
To decorate:
150 ml/¼ pint double cream, whipped
grated chocolate
angelica

AMERICAN
1 × 8 inch cornflake pie shell (see
 page 12)
Filling:
⅔ cup soft brown sugar
½ cup all-purpose flour
2 cups milk
2 egg yolks
2 tablespoons butter
½ teaspoon vanilla extract
To decorate:
⅔ cup heavy cream, whipped
grated chocolate
angelica

Place the brown sugar, flour and milk in a saucepan and heat, stirring, until the sauce thickens, then cook gently for 2 to 3 minutes. Remove from the heat and stir in the egg yolks. Cook for 1 minute, then add the butter and vanilla essence (extract). Pour into the prepared flan case (pie shell) and leave to cool. Chill in the refrigerator before decorating with the whipped cream, chocolate and angelica.

Chestnut Flan (Pie)

METRIC/IMPERIAL
1 × 20 cm/8 inch French flan pastry
 case (see page 11)
Filling:
2 eggs, separated
100 g/4 oz caster sugar
50 g/2 oz butter
225 g/8 oz chestnut purée

AMERICAN
1 × 8 inch French pie dough shell
 (see page 11)
Filling:
2 eggs, separated
½ cup sugar
¼ cup butter
1 cup chestnut purée

Beat together the egg yolks and sugar until pale and creamy. Soften the butter and blend in first the chestnut purée and then the egg yolks and sugar.

Whisk the egg whites until stiff and fold into the chestnut purée mixture. Pour into the prepared flan case (pie shell) and bake in a preheated moderately hot oven (190°C/375°F, Gas Mark 5) for 45 minutes. Serve warm.

BUTTERSCOTCH FLAN (PIE) (*Photograph: Milk Marketing Board*)

Tartellette Coeur à la Crème

METRIC/IMPERIAL
1 × 20 cm/8 inch shortbread flan
  pastry case (see page 15)
Filling:
225 g/8 oz soft cream cheese
2 tablespoons caster sugar
½ teaspoon vanilla essence
150 ml/¼ pint double cream
few red cherries, stoned, to decorate

AMERICAN
1 × 8 inch shortbread pie dough shell
  (see page 15)
Filling:
1 cup soft cream cheese
2 tablespoons sugar
½ teaspoon vanilla extract
⅔ cup heavy cream
few red cherries, pitted, to decorate

Sieve (strain) the cream cheese into a bowl, then beat in the sugar, vanilla essence (extract) and cream. Spoon the mixture into the prepared flan case (pie shell) and decorate with the red cherries. Serve chilled.

Frangipane Flan (Pie)

METRIC/IMPERIAL
1 × 20 cm/8 inch nut flan case (see
  page 14)
Filling:
25 g/1 oz cornflour
450 ml/¾ pint milk
4 egg yolks
25 g/1 oz caster sugar
75 g/3 oz ground almonds
100 g/4 oz green grapes, skinned,
  halved and seeded
2 oranges, peeled and segmented
1 banana, peeled and sliced
50 g/2 oz toasted flaked almonds to
  decorate

AMERICAN
1 × 8 inch nut pie shell (see page
  14)
Filling:
¼ cup cornstarch
2 cups milk
4 egg yolks
2 tablespoons sugar
¾ cup ground almonds
1 cup white grapes, skinned, halved
  and seeded
2 oranges, peeled and segmented
1 banana, peeled and sliced
½ cup toasted flaked almonds to
  decorate

Blend the cornflour (cornstarch) to a smooth paste with a little of the milk. Heat the remaining milk until almost boiling then add to the cornflour (cornstarch). Stir well and return to the pan. Heat, stirring continuously, until the custard thickens.

Remove from the heat and gradually beat in the egg yolks. Cook over a gentle heat for 4 minutes. Remove from the heat and stir in the sugar and ground almonds. Cover and leave until cold.

Arrange the grapes, oranges and banana in the prepared flan case (pie shell). Beat the cooled frangipane cream until smooth, and spread over the fruit. Decorate with the flaked almonds.

Walnut Flan (Pie)

METRIC/IMPERIAL

1 × 20 cm/8 inch French flan pastry
   case (see page 11)

Filling:
75 g/3 oz butter
175 g/6 oz soft brown sugar
2 eggs, beaten
100 g/4 oz walnuts, chopped
½ teaspoon vanilla essence
few whole walnuts to decorate

AMERICAN

1 × 8 inch French pie dough shell
   (see page 11)

Filling:
6 tablespoons butter
1 cup soft brown sugar
2 eggs, beaten
1 cup chopped walnuts
½ teaspoon vanilla extract
few whole walnuts to decorate

Cream together the butter and sugar in a bowl until light and fluffy. Gradually beat in the eggs, then fold in the walnuts and vanilla essence (extract). Spoon the mixture into the prepared flan case (pie shell) and bake in a preheated moderately hot oven (200°C/400°F, Gas Mark 6) for 15 to 20 minutes. Decorate with the walnuts and serve warm with lightly whipped or soured (sour) cream.

Prune and Soured (Sour) Cream Flan (Pie)

METRIC/IMPERIAL

1 × 20 cm/8 inch shortcrust pastry or
   cornflake crust flan case (see page
   10/12)

Filling:
350 g/12 oz dried prunes
600 ml/1 pint cold water
2 eggs, beaten
100 g/4 oz soft brown sugar
150 ml/¼ pint soured cream
150 ml/¼ pint double cream to decorate

AMERICAN

1 × 8 inch basic pie dough or
   cornflake crust shell (see page
   10/12)

Filling:
¾ lb dried prunes
1¼ cups cold water
2 eggs, beaten
⅔ cup soft brown sugar
⅔ cup sour cream
⅔ cup heavy cream to decorate

Soak the prunes in the water overnight, then drain and reserve the liquid. Remove the stones (seeds) from the prunes and chop the flesh.

   Place the reserved liquid in a saucepan and reduce to 4 tablespoons. Add the prunes to the liquid with the eggs, sugar and soured (sour) cream, then heat, stirring continuously, for 10 minutes until the mixture thickens. Allow to cool, then spoon into the prepared flan case (pie shell). Chill in the refrigerator.

   Whip the cream until thick and use to decorate the flan (shell).

INDEX

NOTES

NOTES

NOTES